EFFECTIVE STRATEGIC PLANNING

A HANDBOOK FOR HUMAN RESOURCE PROFESSIONALS

By Christine D. Keen
Edited by Michael R. Losey, SPHR

Society for Human Resource Management
Alexandria, Virginia

SOCIETY FOR

HUMAN

RESOURCE

MANAGEMENT

TABLE OF CONTENTS

INTRODUCTION
WHY STRATEGIC PLANNING FOR HR PROFESSIONALS?

Changes in the business world require an unprecedented alignment of human resource professionals with top business officers—dynamic new partnerships formed to map out long-term organizational planning strategies in an era when the path to success is in constant flux. As never before, new economic pressures from global competition, political activity, social change, technological improvements and an increasingly costly and more diverse white collar workforce require persistent updating of strategic planning maps leading to bottom-line success. Human resource managers must play key roles in this process.

This approach is quite different from past technical and academic writings about the emerging world of human resource strategic planning. Such insight has not been terribly meaningful to the hundreds of thousands of serious-minded human resource professionals with limited time and resources to participate intelligently in the strategic planning. We need more than pearls of wisdom. We need tangible help not only to get our jobs done today but to find time and a way to plan for tomorrow.

Effective Strategic Planning: A Handbook for Human Resource Professionals does more than provide an academic description about strategic planning. This handbook helps the human resource manager derive how-to answers to get the strategic planning job done.

Strategic planning should be a top priority for the human resource department of every company, big or small, public or private. Participation in the strategic planning process—be it for the organization as a whole or for the HR department itself—provides an excellent opportunity for human resource professionals to contribute to the success of both their companies and their departments. Even plans that individuals may develop but keep locked in a desk drawer serve a useful purpose by helping human resource professionals identify, for themselves, where they are and where they need to go.

To do this, though, requires enough discipline to take time out from the pressures of a busy day to explore values and priorities, to challenge past assumptions and to consider new opportunities outside the traditional "boxes." For many human resource professionals, finding the time and winding their way through the process is no easy task. For this reason, *Effective Strategic Planning* is designed to serve as your guide, providing time-tested ideas to help busy HR professionals attack the strategic planning process a step at a time. How do you identify internal and external issues that are important to the future of the organization? How do you assess if you and your organization are likely to benefit from strategic planning? How do you build consensus for an organizational vision of the future? How do you write effective goals and objectives? How do you measure success?

The strategies contained in this handbook can be used in a variety of situations in ways that are easy to understand and implement by the human resource generalist as well as the specialist. Used with the companion book, *Emerging Issues in Human Resources: Looking at the Workplace of Tomorrow Today*, this guide provides the human resource professional with a practical, straightforward model for strategic planning as well as the ammunition necessary to ensure human resource managers get a seat at the table.

Human resource departments bring a unique—and critical—perspective to the strategic planning process: the human side of the business equation. All too often, the rest of the management team forgets that even the most brilliant strategic plan will not succeed without the energy and the commitment of the organization's people.

The more than 60,000 members of the Society for Human Resource Management include human resource professionals from firms of all types and sizes, from Fortune 500 to firms with fewer than 100 people. All share a common goal: to bring their unique perspective to bear in helping their organizations chart a successful course in a sometimes topsy-turvy world. We hope these handbooks help you further this goal.

Michael R. Losey, SPHR
President and CEO, Society for Human Resource Management
Alexandria, VA
May 1994

SECTION 1
WHAT IS "STRATEGIC PLANNING"?

Without a doubt, "strategic" has become one of the most over-used, yet poorly understood, words in the executive vocabulary. Consequently, confusion about what it means to be "strategic" has only added to the confusion about what it means to do "strategic planning." This handbook will attempt to clear up some of this confusion by explaining what strategic planning is, why strategic planning is done and how you may be able to use strategic planning in your own organization.

The term "strategic planning" has its roots in World War II military planning techniques and began appearing in corporate settings by the 1960s. Over the last three decades, strategic planning has evolved into a management discipline taught in most business schools as well as a specific process for articulating an organization's long-term goals and its plans for achieving those goals.* This handbook will focus on the process of strategic planning.

Before describing what strategic planning *is*, it is important to note what it is *not*: strategic planning is not the same as financial planning, scenario building, operational planning, future forecasting or economic modeling, for example—although many organizations use these techniques in strategic planning.

DEFINING "STRATEGIC"

To talk about "strategic planning," one must first define "strategic."

"Strategic" means working from a strategy. A strategy is a specific plan of action designed to achieve a specific objective. The objective is usually long range and cen-

---

*The term "organization" is used throughout this text for simplicity's sake, but strategic planning can also be done by individuals (for personal or professional use) or by any group within a larger organization (*e.g.*, work teams, staff functions, business units). An HR department, for example, can develop its own strategic plan, articulating its own long-term goals and its plans for achieving them. For a sample HR department strategic planning "shell," see the Appendix.

tral to the organization's mission and/or its ability to carry out that mission.

Chess players, for example, employ strategies. Rather than merely moving their pieces randomly around the board, chess players move their pieces in such a way as to advance specific objectives (*e.g.*, capturing an opponent's rook or forcing an opponent into check). The individual moves (or "tactics") are part of the player's broader game plan (or "strategy") and reflect the player's individual priorities (*e.g.*, is it more important to capture a knight or a bishop? would I rather sacrifice a rook or three pawns?). Both players must be continually aware of not only their own strengths and vulnerabilities but also those of their opponent. As the game unfolds, the players' strategies will change to capitalize on new opportunities or minimize potential threats.

The example of a chess game highlights some of the key features of strategic planning:

- Strategies are not just a random sequence of actions; they are a sequence of actions designed to achieve specific objectives.
- These strategic objectives may be either short term or long term, but they are critical to long-term success.
- The development of a given strategy reflects the strategist's personal values and priorities; the development of a group strategy should, therefore, reflect the group's values and priorities.
- Effective execution of a given strategy requires an understanding of both internal strengths and weaknesses as well as external threats and opportunities.
- Strategic planning is a dynamic process and requires regular "reality checks."

OBJECTIVES OF STRATEGIC PLANNING

Strategic planning is a process for (1) articulating an organization's values and long-range goals and (2) developing the strategies necessary to achieve these goals. Put another way, strategic planning is the organization's route from "is" to "should be." Consequently, the primary objectives of strategic planning are to assess what "is," decide what "should be" and develop a series of strategies for advancing the organization from "is" to "should be."

All good planning is grounded in the truth. Therefore, in assessing what "is," strategic planning requires an accurate picture of both an organization's *internal* resources and capabilities as well as the *external* environment in which it operates. Often, one of the biggest obstacles in strategic planning is not what you *don't* know but what you think you *do* know. Therefore, the first steps in the strategic planning process require you to take a critical look at both internal resources and the external environment, revisiting assumptions and updating old information.

The third step in strategic planning tackles what is frequently the most difficult part of the process: deciding what "should be." Of all the *possible* futures, which is the organization's *preferred* future? An organization's decisions about its preferred future will depend on its values and priorities and will, in turn, determine its strategic objectives and its plan for achieving them.

Finally, after an organization has reached consensus about where it is and where it would like to go, it needs to develop a plan for getting from here to there. What are the specific things the organization must do to get from where it is today to where it wants to be in the future? Who is going to do these things and when must they be done? Strategic planning is more than a simple "visioning" exercise about the future—its end product is a specific plan with specific timetables and accountabilities.

BENEFITS OF STRATEGIC PLANNING

Organizations use strategic planning because of its perceived benefits. The most commonly cited benefits of strategic planning are highlighted below.

- Strategic planning improves organizational performance.

    By forcing an organization to articulate where it would like to go and then establishing specific objectives, priorities, action steps, timetables and accountability, strategic planning allows an organization to focus its resources for maximum long-term impact.

- Strategic planning can minimize "management by crisis."

    Organizations that manage by crisis tend to do a poor job of anticipating future needs and are often caught unprepared. Strategic planning provides a process for engaging the organization in thinking about—and spelling out—future needs and priorities.

- Strategic planning serves as an "early warning system," alerting an organization to potential threats or opportunities from within or beyond the organization.

    By identifying these issues early, the organization can develop plans to capitalize on—or minimize—the impact of emerging change.

- Strategic planning provides a mechanism for building in continuous quality improvements and assigning accountability for results.

    By incorporating the action plan developed as part of the strategic planning process into the organization's operational plan, day-to-day operations can be linked directly with long-term performance objectives.

- Strategic planning can serve as the basis of an organization's performance appraisal system.

    By tying individual performance objectives to the organization's strategic objectives, the organization can create an explicit reward system that recognizes achievement in support of the organization's strategic goals.

- Finally, the process of developing a strategic plan is often a valuable team-building exercise.

    Strategic planning gives team members an all-too-rare opportunity to discuss "big picture" plans and priorities. These discussions themselves can often improve an organization's thinking about the future and help build consensus for—and ownership of—organizational goals.

SECTION I WORKSHEET
IS STRATEGIC PLANNING FOR YOU?

The worksheets at the end of each section are designed to help you build the foundations for your own departmental strategic planning. Before you begin, though, you might find it useful to assess the "strategic planning readiness" of your department.

Do you, personally, know what you want to be doing in three years?

❑ No.
(0)

❑ Sort of.
(1)

❑ Definitely.
(2)

Do you have specific work goals for next year?

❑ No.
(0)

❑ I have an idea of what
(1) I should be working on
next year.

❑ I have written goals for
(2) next year.

Does your department have specific work goals for next year?

❑ No.
(0)

❑ My department has an
(1) idea of what we will be
working on next year.

❑ My department has
(2) written goals for
next year.

Does your organization do strategic planning?

❑ No.
(0)

❑ Yes, but I'm not involved.
(1)

❑ Yes and I am involved.
(2)

Could your staff members explain how their work fits into the organization's long-term plans?

❑ The organization doesn't
(0) have long-term plans.

❑ Some of my staff
(1) members could explain
how their work fits into
the organization's
long-term plans.

❑ All of my staff members
(2) could explain how
their work fits into the
organization's long-term
plans.

Does your department have a "mission statement"?

❑ No.
(0)

❑ We have an
(1) understanding of
what our mission is.

❑ We have a written
(2) "mission statement."

Could you identify your department's "values"?

❏   I don't understand the   ❏   I think I could.   ❏   We have developed
(0)   question.   (1)   (2)   a written statement of
                                                                           values.

Could your department break away from day-to-day concerns to devote five full days to planning for the future?

❏   No.   ❏   Maybe.   ❏   Definitely, this is
(0)   (1)   (2)   important.

Add up the points below each box you checked.

If your score is 0–8: Your department would no doubt benefit from strategic planning, but because it is likely to be a significant departure from the way you and your staff usually do things, you should seriously evaluate the level of commitment—both yours and theirs—before beginning, particularly if you scored 0 points for either the first or the last question.

If your score is 9–12: Your department is likely to be familiar with at least the rudiments of strategic planning, even if the term itself is not used. Done well, strategic planning could be of considerable benefit to your department, and this handbook may be most useful to you as a first-time guide to the process.

If your score is 13–16: Your department is probably already doing strategic planning or something like it. This handbook may be most useful to you as a source of "tips" to help you refine or restructure your process.

If you and your department were to go through the strategic planning process, what would you like to get out of it?

_____

_____

_____

_____

_____

_____

_____

_____

_____

SECTION II
IDENTIFYING THE COMPONENTS OF STRATEGIC PLANNING

Planning is a process we use all the time, whether we realize it or not. Every time we come up with a "to do" list, for example, we are assessing what "is," identifying what "should be" and deciding what we need to do to get from here to there. The same basic process applies to strategic planning.

Strategic planning has six key components, each of which is highlighted below and explored in greater detail in the remaining sections of this handbook. The first two components (the internal and external scans) help the organization assess what "is." The third component (the vision and purpose statements) helps the organization decide what "should be." The last three components (identifying objectives, developing an action plan and evaluating progress) help the organization decide what it needs to do to get from "is" to "should be."

- Internal Scan: Understanding Your Resources
  In order to plan for the future, you need to know what your resources are right now. In strategic planning, the internal scan is designed to help an organization identify its current resources (physical, financial, human, attitudinal, etc.) and assess how those resources may be strengths or weaknesses for the organization.

- External Scan: Assessing Your Environment
  Internal resources are only part of the planning equation, though. You also need to know what's going on around you and how that might affect your plans. The external scan is designed to alert an organization to what is going on in its external environment and how these actual or anticipated events may translate into challenges or opportunities for the organization. (Because it deals with the external environment, the external scan is sometimes known as the "environmental scan.")

▪ Vision and Purpose Statements: Articulating Your Preferred Future

Planning requires a specific target: you have to know where you want to go before you can decide how to get there. The vision and purpose statements serve as this "target" for strategic planning. By articulating its "preferred future," an organization can begin developing a specific action plan to make that future happen.

▪ Strategic Objectives: Outlining Key Objectives for Securing That Future

The process of setting key objectives forces an organization to identify those issues that will be most critical to making its preferred future a reality. These objectives tend to be broadly stated (*e.g.*, improve customer service) and refer to *what* must be done, not *how* to do it.

▪ Action Plan: Deciding Who Must Do What When to Achieve Those Objectives

Key objectives describe *what* must be done; the action plan describes *how* these things will be done. The action plan lays out the specific tasks necessary to achieve a given objective and assigns timetables and accountability for these tasks.

▪ Evaluating Progress: Deciding If Your Plan Is Working

Planning is a dynamic process that requires regular evaluation. Is your plan working? Is there something you've forgotten? Has anything in the internal or external environment changed that requires you to change your plan? Are timetables being met? Strategic plans that are put in nice binders and placed on shelves to collect dust do little good. An organization's strategic plan should be a living document that reflects the organization's personality, purpose, plans, priorities and progress.

The remaining six sections of this handbook describe, in detail, each of these six components of strategic planning.

SECTION II WORKSHEET
COMPONENTS OF STRATEGIC PLANNING

Many organizations have gone through various parts of the strategic planning process at one time or another, with varying levels of success. Before you begin your strategic planning, it may be useful to identify which components of the process—and which sections of this handbook—you may want to concentrate on.

1.   **Has your department done a formal internal scan within the last two years?**

  No.   Yes.

 If "yes," how satisfied were you with the results?
  Very satisfied.   Mostly satisfied—   Mostly unsatisfied.
            room for improvement.

What would you like to do better or differently?_____
_____
_____
_____

2.   **Has your department done a formal external scan within the last two years?**

  No.   Yes.

 If "yes," how satisfied were you with the results?
  Very satisfied.   Mostly satisfied—   Mostly unsatisfied.
            room for improvement.

What would you like to do better or differently?_____
_____
_____
_____

3.   **Has your department written a formal vision statement and/or purpose statement within the last two years?**

  No.   Yes.

 If "yes," how satisfied were you with the results?
  Very satisfied.   Mostly satisfied—   Mostly unsatisfied.
            room for improvement.

What would you like to do better or differently?_____

_____

_____

_____

4.   **Has your department developed key objectives for the future within the last two years?**

❑ No.   ❑ Yes.

If "yes," how satisfied were you with the results?

❑ Very satisfied.   ❑ Mostly satisfied—   ❑ Mostly unsatisfied.
                                 room for improvement.

What would you like to do better or differently?_____

_____

_____

_____

5.   **Has your department developed an action plan with specific goals for the future within the last two years?**

❑ No.   ❑ Yes.

If "yes," how satisfied were you with the results?

❑ Very satisfied.   ❑ Mostly satisfied—   ❑ Mostly unsatisfied.
                                 room for improvement.

What would you like to do better or differently?_____

_____

_____

_____

6.   **Has your department tried to measure its progress against a written plan within the last two years?**

❑ No.   ❑ Yes.

If "yes," how satisfied were you with the results?

❑ Very satisfied.   ❑ Mostly satisfied—   ❑ Mostly unsatisfied.
                                 room for improvement.

What would you like to do better or differently?_____
_____
_____
_____

SECTION III
CONDUCTING AN INTERNAL SCAN

The scope of an organization's strategic planning depends on two things: its resources and its ability and willingness to change.

If an organization has few resources, it may be able to do only a few things at a time, making its planning relatively simple. More importantly, if an organization is not willing or able to change, there is no point in developing elaborate plans for the future because they will not be implemented. Conducting an internal scan helps an organization assess both its resources and its change-ability.

DEVELOPING A "RISK-TAKING QUOTIENT"

One way to assess an organization's change-ability is to calculate its "risk-taking quotient." A "risk-taking quotient" (RTQ) measures how comfortable the organization is with risk. A simple exercise for doing an RTQ is illustrated below.

"On a scale of 1 to 10 (with 1=risk averse and 10=risk seeker), where do you think you are? (Would your friends/co-workers agree?)"

1	2	3	4	5	6	7	8	9	10
risk averse									**risk seeker**

This simple self-assessment tool can be done anonymously or as a group. The group's results should be displayed throughout the planning process. In a group of eight people, for example, the results can vary widely.

Group A

1	2	3	4	5	6	7	8	9	10
risk averse									**risk seeker**

Group B

1	2	3	4	5	6	7	8	9	10
risk averse									**risk seeker**

Although the average score for these two groups is roughly the same, the "personalities" of the groups appear quite different. Group A may have a more difficult time reaching a consensus, for example, but Group B may have a more difficult time moving away from "business as usual."

> *If time and resources permit, you can also do an RTQ with a Myers-Briggs or similar personality indicator. For strategic planning purposes, focus on the areas of the test that deal with individuals' attitudes toward change. Doing a broader personality assessment, like a Myers-Briggs, may tie in with other organizational development work that the HR department is already undertaking.*

In doing an internal scan, it is important to assess the risk-taking quotient of at least three groups: the planning group, the group that will have to "sign off" on the plan (*e.g.*, senior managers) and the group that will have to implement the plan (*e.g.*, middle-managers, first-line supervisors and employees). Each of these groups has a distinct but critical stake in the plan, and understanding where differences of opinion are likely to arise can help pinpoint potential problems and encourage realistic goal setting.

In evaluating your results, consider the following specific areas: What is the RTQ of your planning group? How does it vary by individual or function? Are there differences between management and the planning group? Or between staff and the planning group? Or between staff and management? How are these differences likely to be a problem for the organization? How can they benefit the organization? What kind of organizational development issues, if any, do the different RTQs suggest?

It is often useful to display the different groups' RTQ results prominently throughout the strategic planning process to remind participants that their point of view is not the only one.

IDENTIFYING INTERNAL RESOURCES AND CAPABILITIES

Identifying internal resources and capabilities is one of the easiest parts of strategic planning, but it also tends to be one of the most frequently ignored—perhaps because everyone thinks they already know the answers. The process of thinking through the questions and discussing the answers, though, is invariably illuminating.

Internal resources and capabilities can be divided into three groups: resources, structures and values. The questions on the worksheet at the end of this section highlight some of the issues that should be addressed within each group. Some of the questions have straightforward answers while others are highly subjective. The answers to the questions are important, but your group's discussion of the questions—and your ability to reach consensus on the answers—is often more important.

These questions are intended to be only a beginning. The objective of the internal scan is to provide as complete a picture as possible of the current state of the organization. You may discover that many of the "answers" raise additional questions and that some areas require further exploration.

You may also discover that this process generates issues that will resurface again when you are discussing the vision and purpose statements. In the meantime, save the "answers" from the internal scan. You will come back to them again later when you are developing the objectives and action plan. (Think of the internal scan as what "is." After you have decided on a preferred future, you will need to re-examine your internal resources and capabilities to determine how they will need to change in order to get you to what "should be.")

SECTION III WORKSHEET
INTERNAL SCAN

To begin the internal scan, try assessing your own "risk-taking quotient" (RTQ):

On a scale of 1 to 10 (with 1=risk averse and 10=risk seeker), where do you think you are? (Would your friends/co-workers agree?)

      1   2   3   4   5   6   7   8   9   10

risk averse   **risk seeker**

Because strategic planning means going beyond "business as usual," if your RTQ is three or lower, you may need to evaluate your own comfort with—and commitment to—change before undertaking a strategic planning project.

On a scale of 1 to 10 (with 1=risk averse and 10=risk seeker), where do you think your boss is?

      1   2   3   4   5   6   7   8   9   10

risk averse   **risk seeker**

Do you think your boss will support a different way of doing things in your department? If you think his or her RTQ is low, you should consider talking with your boss beforehand to ensure that he or she is comfortable with the idea and will support the process and its results.

On a scale of 1 to 10 (with 1=risk averse and 10=risk seeker), where do you think your key staff members are?

      1   2   3   4   5   6   7   8   9   10

risk averse   **risk seeker**

Unless you're willing to do the strategic planning—and the implementation—by yourself, you need to consider your staff's willingness to give up "business as usual." If you intend to introduce the idea of doing departmental strategic planning, you may want to begin with an RTQ exercise for your staff. (Were your perceptions accurate? If not, why not?)

The kinds of issues you address in an internal scan will depend on your department and your organization. The questions below provide a framework to begin the process, but don't forget: this is only a starting point. Try to encourage full discussion of the questions and their "answers."

RESOURCES

Financial resources

What is our annual revenue? (Is there a trend line?)

Where does the money come from?

What are our annual expenses? (Is there a trend line?)

Where does the money go?

Human resources

What is our current staffing level?

How is this staffing deployed (by function or sub-unit)?

What percentage of staff is full-time? part-time? temporary? male? female? union? non-union? on-site? off-site? etc.

What is our current payroll and total compensation costs?

How is this payroll distributed across the department?

What would a "skill map" of the department look like? (Who has what kind of skill/knowledge/expertise?)

Do we have human resources at our disposal that are not reflected by the payroll (e.g., volunteers, board members, consultants)?

Technology

Is our technology (e.g., hardware, software, telecommunications systems) state-of-the art?

If not, how many "generations" old is it?

Is our technology at least sufficient to satisfy our customers' needs and expectations?

Leadership

Where are "leaders" within the department?

What is the staff's view of senior management?

Image

How is the department viewed by our customers (including employees, the CEO and other department heads)?

How is the department viewed in the community (by union leaders, our peers in other organizations, etc.)?

How does the department view itself?

STRUCTURES

Physical structure

Where is our worksite located? Why?

Is our worksite in good repair?

Is our worksite safe and secure?

Are the space and configuration suitable for our needs?

Social structure

What are the lines of command within the department?

What are the (formal and informal) lines of communication within the department?

VALUES

Organizational values

What are three things the department rewards people for?

What are three things the department penalizes people for?

How does the department define "ethical" behavior?

Management values

How would you describe the management style most prevalent in the department?

How does management style vary (by function, by sub-unit or by individual)?

What are three things you think the department head values?

What are three things you think department supervisors value?

What are three things you think other employees value?

SECTION IV
CONDUCTING AN EXTERNAL SCAN

If the internal scan looks at issues in the organization's *internal* operating environment, the external scan looks at issues in the organization's *external* operating environment. Yet at any given time, hundreds or even thousands of issues are swirling around the organization. How do you identify which issues are important and what their impact might be?

The external scan is a way of assessing what is going on in an organization's external environment and how these actual or anticipated events might affect the organization. An external scan has three objectives: to identify external issues important to the organization, to forecast how these issues might grow or change during the planning horizon (*e.g.*, over the next three years) and to analyze the possible implications of these issues for the organization.

Typically, external issues are grouped into four categories:

- economic
- political
- social
- technological

Economic issues, as the name implies, deal with economic trends and events. Sample economic issues might have to do with unemployment, interest rates, economic growth, taxes, productivity, input costs or exchange rates. Or economic issues might deal with "big picture" economic issues like the shift from manufacturing to information employment or the emergence of international markets for goods and services. The economic issues you need to look at will depend on your organization. (If you are doing a strategic plan for your HR department, for example, you might not care about interest rates, but changes in benefits costs might be very important. The scope of your external scan needs to be adapted to the organization or unit you are doing planning for.)

Political issues deal with legislation, regulations and court cases as well as issues affecting individual policymakers or the overall political environment. What kind of political issues is the organization dealing with now? What kinds of political issues are likely to come up in the future? How might these political issues affect the organization during the planning period?

Social issues deal with social values, lifestyles and demographics. Many political issues, in fact, begin as social issues. (Long before being proposed as legislation, family leave laws, for example, were preceded by changes in values, lifestyles and demographics.) Social issues might be quantitative (like trends in birth rates or the proportion of Asians in the population) or they might be qualitative (like perceptions about having too little time or less commitment between employees and employers).

Technological issues deal with changes in technology and work processes. What is new in information technology, for example, or factory automation equipment? Do these changes in technology suggest parallel changes in the way work is done or business is conducted? How might these actual or anticipated changes affect your organization?

Not all issues fit neatly into these four categories, and there is no need to "squeeze" them into one category or another. These four issue areas are intended to be a beginning, not necessarily an end. The point of doing an external scan is to identify those issues likely to affect the organization, in one way or another, during the planning horizon. It is better to start with too many issues and whittle them down than to restrict thinking only to those issues that fit neatly into one of the four scanning categories.

DEVELOPING AN ISSUE MATRIX

In order to help provide a framework for looking at external issues, some planners use an "issue matrix." An issue matrix is designed to help planners identify issues emerging in different parts of the organization's external operating environment. An example of an issue matrix is sketched out below.

	customers	industry	business world	community	nation	world
economic						
political						
social						
technological						

Each of the "boxes" points to a different area of the organization's external environment. What are the economic issues affecting your customers, for example? What are the political issues affecting your industry? What are the technological issues affecting the business world? What are the social issues affecting your community? Take a minute and try coming up with at least three "answers" for each of these questions.

The advantage of the issue matrix is that it requires the planning group to think about the organization's external environment in a very structured way, often producing a very comprehensive scan. The disadvantage of the issue matrix is that the "boxes" can limit participants' thinking. Individuals may be reluctant to nominate issues because they may be unsure where an issue "fits," if it fits.

One way around this problem is to do the external scan in two steps: using an initial "brainstorming" session to encourage participants to list any issue they think may be important; then, in a second session, using the issue matrix to identify how the issues raised in the initial session might fit into the matrix and to identify "gaps" that require further discussion.

> *The greater the diversity of opinions, the more complete a picture the external scan will provide. If you suspect your group might have problems with "group think" or with a handful of dominant personalities, you might want to consider doing at least part of the initial nomination of issues anonymously, using either an interactive computer system or pencil and paper. Participants can then discuss and add to this initial listing as a group.*

Some "boxes" in the matrix may contain 20 or more issues when completed. Others may contain only a handful. The planning group itself should be a rich source of information about what is going on in the external environment. In some instances, though, you may decide you want to supplement the list the planning group comes up with. In this case, you may want to ask other experts in the field what they think or work with an external consultant to help you identify important issues. You may also want to commission a series of focus groups to find out what customers or community members think is important.

Just as you would not want to plan a road trip using an old map, so the key to developing a useful external scan is ensuring that the planning group is working with the best available "intelligence" about the external environment and its implications for the future of the organization.

FORECASTING THE FUTURE OF YOUR ISSUES

The second step in doing an external scan is to forecast how the issues you identified in the first stage of the scan are likely to change during the planning horizon. Strategic planning, by its very nature, requires you to "hit a moving target." If you are doing planning for 1997, for example, you need to be able to anticipate how the world in which you are doing business will look in 1997.

Therefore, you need to be able to forecast how the issues that you identified earlier may change by 1997. Which issues will have grown more important? Which will have faded? How might the issues develop, shift focus or be resolved by 1997?

You don't have a crystal ball, but you do have a variety of other future forecasting methods at your disposal. One approach, of course, is to ask people their opinions. You can ask members of your planning group what they think the future of these external issues may look like. You can ask other experts in the field. You can ask specialists who deal with demographics or economics or politics. Or you can ask those people who may be in a position to influence the issues you are interested in: customers, employees, community activists, policymakers, union leaders, etc.

Everyone is likely to have an opinion about the future. In assessing your group's responses, you will need to examine several factors:

- Where are there areas of consensus?
- Where is there disagreement?
- What are the different assumptions people are using in making their forecasts?
- Whose opinions are more likely to be "right" and should be weighted more heavily?

Based on the answers you receive, you will be able to develop a "composite" forecast of how the issues you have identified might look during your planning horizon.

A formal forecasting technique using a similar approach is known as Delphi. Delphi techniques ask a group of experts to first nominate possible future events and then to vote (anonymously) on these issues' probability and importance to the organization. The group continues to discuss—and re-vote on—these issues until consensus is reached about "the future." (How probable is each event? How important is each event to the organization? How confident is the group in its opinion? Etc.)

A second approach to forecasting is to do some research. What do the data actually look like? What has been written about the future of your issues?

You may find that the data do not support the conventional wisdom about your issues. Digging through industry or government statistics may help give you an understanding of the history of your issues. From an understanding of their history, you may be able to make some educated guesses about their future. (Note: the statistics themselves are less useful indicators of the future than are the underlying forces creating the statistics. Instead of doing a simple extrapolation of the numbers, you need to consider the underlying forces: What are they? Do you expect that they will intensify, dissipate or change direction over time?)

Literature searches—either by doing regular "scans" of the relevant literature or by spending some time in the library once a year—may also shed some light on the future of your issues. What are other people saying and writing about them? Why do they arrive at the conclusions they do? Are their views credible? Based on your research, you should be able to present your group with either an array of opinions or a composite forecast based on the views you consider most likely.

A third approach to forecasting your issues is to hire a firm that specializes in future forecasting. An outside firm can help you identify important issues and develop forecasts for these issues. An outside firm can offer a valuable perspective on your issues, but in evaluating their conclusions, you need to ask yourself: How did they arrive at their conclusions? What were their sources of information? What are the implicit or explicit assumptions used in making a particular forecast? Are their assumptions and conclusions credible?

When you have identified the external issues likely to impact your organization and you have forecast what they might look like during the period for which you are planning, the last step in doing an external scan is to analyze the implications of these issues for the organization.

ANALYZING THE IMPLICATIONS OF YOUR ISSUES FOR THE ORGANIZATION

Let's say, for example, that in step 1, you identified "growing concern about workplace violence" as one of the social issues in your community. Then in step 2, you forecast that, during your planning period, this issue will still be around and that, in fact, there may be more public pressure for firms to protect their employees or for holding firms responsible for failing to do so. Now in step 3, you decide what the implications of these developments may be for your organization.

Is this issue and its anticipated future a threat or an opportunity for your organization? How big of an impact is it likely to have? How big of an impact *could* it have if the firm takes action one way or another?

In answering these questions, some planners use an impact-probability chart like the one below. By assigning each issue an impact and a probability, an impact-probability chart helps graphically represent where your biggest problems and opportunities may lie.

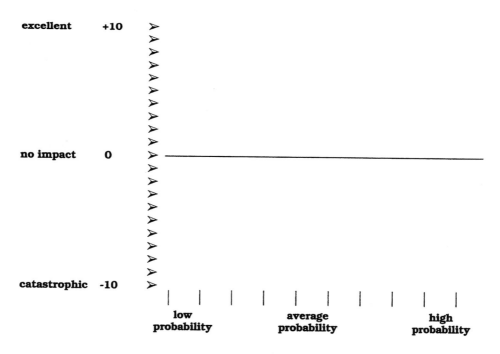

How would you rate the impact on your organization of an episode of workplace violence? How probable is an episode of workplace violence during your planning horizon? How would you rate the impact on your organization of OSHA regulations dealing with workplace violence? How probable are OSHA regulations dealing with workplace violence during your planning horizon?

By estimating the impact and probability of each of the issues identified earlier, your planning group can identify, for example, the most probable events or those with the greatest impact (positive or negative).

To date, though, your external scan is only descriptive: it describes the external environment in which your organization will be doing business during the planning period. The final external scanning task—and the one most critical to planning—is to turn this information from *descriptive* into *prescriptive:* based on the things you have identified in the external environment, what can your organization do to minimize the probability of a negative issue, increase the probability of a positive issue, or make any issue a bit more positive for the organization?

These recommendations will come into play when you are setting key objectives and developing an action plan. For now, though, you will need to switch gears and begin exploring how the organization defines itself and its purpose.

SECTION IV WORKSHEET
EXTERNAL SCAN

To begin the external scan, ask members of your staff to supply their thoughts for the questions below. Compile their answers and use this as the basis for group discussion.

What are 3 *economic* issues you think might be important to the future of the department?

_____

_____

_____

What are 3 *political* issues you think might be important to the future of the department?

_____

_____

_____

What are 3 *social* issues you think might be important to the future of the department?

_____

_____

_____

What are 3 *technological* issues you think might be important to the future of the department?

_____

_____

_____

When group members have discussed each other's responses to the questions above and have nominated and discussed any additional issues they think relevant for the external scan, ask each of them to "vote" for 10 that they believe are most important to the department's future. Tabulate the votes. Is there consensus? Is more discussion needed?

Take the top 15 issues, and ask the group to plot them on an impact-probability chart (see next page). How probable is it that Issue #1, for example, will impact the department during the planning period? How positive or negative is that impact likely to be?

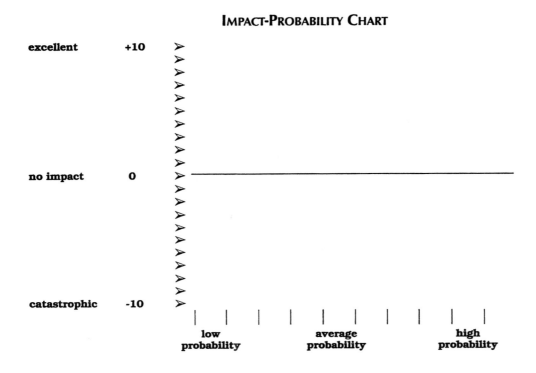

Based on the results of your impact-probability chart, which issue does your group think will have the most *positive* impact on the department? What are two things the department can do to increase its probability?

_____

_____

_____

Based on the results of your impact-probability chart, which issue does your group think will have the most *negative* impact on the department? What are two things the department can do to decrease its probability?

_____

_____

_____

Based on the results of your impact-probability chart, which issue does your group think has the highest probability of impacting the department? What are two things the department can do to make this impact more positive?

_____

_____

_____

NOTE: This same process can be used for evaluating issues that surfaced during the internal scan.

SECTION V
DEVELOPING A VISION AND PURPOSE STATEMENT

"Would you tell me please which way I ought to go from here?"
"That depends a good deal on where you want to get to," said the Cat.
"I don't much care where—" said Alice.
"Then it doesn't much matter which way you go," said the Cat.
— from Alice's Adventures in Wonderland

"Vision" is perhaps as over-used and misunderstood a word as "strategy." Yet without a vision, particularly a shared vision, organizations move into the future without a clear sense of where they are going and why.

As discussed earlier, strategic planning is the process for moving an organization from "is" to "should be." The internal and external scans are designed to help an organization identify what "is." The vision and purpose statements are designed to help an organization articulate what "should be."

Therefore, the next step in strategic planning is to determine what "should be." That vision of what "should be" serves as our target: all of our objectives and action steps should move the group closer to that target.

This section of the handbook will cover vision and purpose statements: what they are, how they are used and the steps involved in writing them.

DEVELOPING A "VISION STATEMENT"

Done well, vision statements are more than simply nice-sounding slogans. They are a distillation of our values, our dreams and our priorities. They are our "stakes in the ground," telling the rest of the world who we are, who we are *not*, what we believe in and who we want to be.

Vision statements should be "gut grabbing." They should galvanize a group and motivate members to put forth their best efforts.

Vision statements **should** be	Vision statements **should not** be
▪ compelling	▪ something that just "sounds" good
▪ easily understood	▪ a slogan
▪ succinct (one or two sentences)	▪ long and involved
▪ enduring	▪ frequently changed
▪ a view of something different, better	▪ a description of operations

*Good Example**	*Bad Example**
"To make a contribution to the world by making tools for the mind that advance humankind." —Steve Jobs Apple Computer	"We provide our customers with retail banking, real estate, finance, and corporate banking products which will meet their credit, investment, security and liquidity needs." —anonymous

Is the example on the right going to get employees out of bed in the morning, eager to come work toward that vision? Steve Jobs' vision for Apple Computer, on the other hand, was compelling enough that in 1984 John Sculley left the top job at Pepsi to become president of Apple Computer after Jobs issued him the now legendary challenge, "Do you want to spend the rest of your life selling sugared water or do you want a chance to change the world?"

Sometimes vision statements are the product of a specific individual (a CEO, an owner, a department head, etc.); other times they are the product of a group. The important feature is not so much who developed the vision statement but that the vision is shared by others.

A group's vision statement is its rallying cry. It tells people where the group wants to go in the future. It welcomes those who want to accompany the group on that journey, and it serves notice to those who do not.

For this reason, vision statements can be both very powerful and very threatening. Vision statements can be powerful when they invigorate a group and focus its

---

*All examples with asterisks are drawn from James C. Collins and Jerry I. Porras, "Organizational Vision and Visionary Organizations," *California Management Review* (Fall 1991), pp. 30–52.

efforts on achieving a specific goal. U.S. President John F. Kennedy, for example, was known for his ability to use a vision statement to mobilize and motivate people. "Ask not what your country can do for you, but what you can do for your country." After a hotly contested election, this simple sentence suddenly captured the imagination of a people, making them feel necessary and involved. It challenged listeners to see themselves and their roles in their communities on a different, higher plane. It launched VISTA, the Peace Corps and thousands of careers in public service.

Similarly, Kennedy's vision of "achieving the goal, before this decade is out, of landing a man on the moon and returning him safely to earth" gave Americans a sense of unlimited aspiration. It was a specific vision of the future, inspiring science and math students to excel, mobilizing support for NASA and expanding America's "manifest destiny" into space. It was not merely a bunch of nice-sounding words strung together.

The power of a compelling vision cannot be underestimated. Ask any religion.

On the other hand, vision statements can be threatening to individuals who either do not share the vision or see themselves excluded from the vision. In many ways, a vision statement is a line in the sand—you are either in support of it or not, a part of it or not. Those individuals who either do not share the vision of a group or believe they are excluded from it may choose to leave the group or may choose to stay and work to undermine it. For the group itself, the latter is definitely worse than the former. (In most cases, it is easier to row a boat with less than a full crew than it is to row a boat with part of the crew rowing in the opposite direction.)

Many organizations, though, either consciously or unconsciously respond to this challenge by "watering down" the vision statement. Unwilling or unable to draw that line in the sand, some groups try to satisfy conflicting ideas about what "should be" by writing a vision statement that is either devoid of real meaning or rambles on long enough to include everyone's pet idea or phrase. (This is particularly true of vision statements written by large groups of people.) A vision statement lacking boldness and clarity may alienate fewer people, but it will also be less effective in guiding and motivating them.

> *If your organization has a vision statement now, do you know what it is? Can you explain what it means and why it is important? If not, chances are other people may not be able to either. Although you may not be able to change the vision statement of the whole organization, you can at least make sure that the part of the organization over which you do have influence—your department, your staff, your own job—has a vision statement of its own that is clear and compelling. If the organization's vision statement doesn't make you hop out of bed in the morning, make sure that your own vision statement does.*

Good vision statements begin with a discussion of core values and guiding philosophies.[**]

CORE VALUES AND GUIDING PHILOSOPHIES

Core values and guiding philosophies are about more than just the business. As one person said in a strategic planning session, they are about "how we are anchored to the cosmos." Core values and guiding philosophies are an articulation of what is important in business and in life. They reflect a view of mankind and of the organization's role in society.

Examples include:

> *"Sell good merchandise at a reasonable price, treat your customers like you would your friends, and the business will take care of itself."*
> —L.L. Bean [*]

> *"See the good in people, and try to develop those qualities."*
> —Marriott [*]

> *"We should always be the pioneers with our products—out front leading the market. We believe in leading the public with new products rather than asking them what kinds of products they want."*
> —Sony [*]

[**] The terms "core values" and "guiding philosophies" are borrowed from Collins and Porras. The use of these terms, however, is slightly different in Collins and Porras than that developed here.

Each of these examples reflects not just what the company believes about itself but also about what is important and about the company's role in the broader society. Often they are the personal values of the founder, but over time every organization needs to re-think and/or re-affirm its core values and guiding philosophies. The strategic planning process is an opportunity to do this.

Unfortunately, you can't just sit people down in a room and ask "So what are your core values and guiding philosophies?" Many of us may not even be aware of them. Others may not feel comfortable talking about them. After all, this is a somewhat unusual topic in a business setting.

The worksheet at the end of this section provides some sample "leading questions" you may be able to use to get the ball rolling.

> *Often discussion of these issues takes hours (or even days). A good facilitator—from within or outside the group—is invaluable. In choosing a facilitator, look for someone with an understanding of what a vision statement is supposed to achieve but without an "agenda" of his or her own. Find someone who is a perceptive listener but not afraid to play "border collie" to bring the group back on track. The ability to provide intelligent answers is less important than the ability to ask intelligent questions.*

This discussion about core values and guiding philosophies should identify those values and philosophies that the organization holds dear. There is no such thing as "correct" core values or guiding philosophies. What is important is to identify yours.

This discussion should lay the groundwork for drafting the vision statement.

What seemed to be the key ideas?

Which ideas and phrases seemed to generate a lot of excitement in the group?

Which ideas and phrases were controversial?

The final step is to distill these ideas into one or two sentences. It will probably take several attempts, but keep in mind that the vision statement undergirds the entire strategic planning process. It will serve as your "banner." It must be easy to understand. It must compel, mobilize, motivate and excite your people. It must understand. It must compel, mobilize, motivate and excite your people. It must have real meaning.

DEVELOPING A "PURPOSE STATEMENT"

"Purpose statements" are also known as "mission statements." But because many people have difficulty distinguishing between "vision" and "mission," this handbook uses the term "purpose statement" instead.

A purpose statement explains the organization's "reason for being" and should answer the question, "Why does this organization exist?" It is both descriptive and prescriptive: it describes the organization as it is now as well as what it aspires to.

Examples of purpose statements:

"I will build a motor car for the great multitude ... it will be so low in price that no man making a good salary will be unable to own one."

—Henry Ford *

"Our mission is to provide the highest quality waste collection, transportation, processing, disposal and related services to both our public and private customers worldwide. We will carry out our mission efficiently, safely and in an environmentally responsible manner and respect the role of government in protecting the public interest."

—Browning-Ferris Industries

"Through the efforts of committed volunteers and an empowered staff, be a recognized world leader in human resource management by: providing high value, high quality, dynamic and responsive programs and service to our customers; being the voice of the profession on workplace issues; [and] guiding the advancement of the human resource profession."

—Society for Human Resource Management

"The Domani Group is committed to providing the best possible analysis of emerging issues and their implications for the future. Our reports, publications and presentations aim to reflect the vision, integrity and insight people have come to expect from members of The Domani Group."

—The Domani Group

As each of these examples show, purpose statements are supportive of, but different from, vision statements. Purpose statements should:

- describe what the organization intends to do to advance its vision of the future;
- explain (broadly) what the organization is in the business of doing and why;
- reflect present and future objectives;
- be revised occasionally as goals are achieved or focuses change;
- be no longer than a paragraph.

Both the vision and the purpose statements need to be future-oriented, "meaty" and motivational, but whereas the vision statement is more internally focused—designed to capture the hearts and minds of people inside the organization—the purpose statement is more externally focused—designed to explain to the outside world who the organization is and what it intends to do.

Many of the same questions used to identify core values and guiding philosophies can also be used to develop a purpose statement. For example, when people first consider "What makes us unique?" they often respond by listing products or services that the organization offers. Only after further questioning do they begin addressing the more fundamental issues of perspective, priorities and other intangible qualities. In developing a purpose statement, though, your products and services are an integral part of who you are and what you do.

To develop a purpose statement, most organizations need to go beyond their discussion of core values and guiding philosophies to explore, on a more down-to-earth level, why they are in business, who their customers are and what they hope to offer them. This process is sometimes referred to as a strategic needs analysis.

CONDUCTING A STRATEGIC NEEDS ANALYSIS

Although it is true that the one thing every business must have is customers, most businesses do not begin with this perspective. Instead, most businesses begin with an idea. It might be an idea about a product or a service or a long-term objective, but most businesses begin, at least in the minds of their founders, as an idea in search of customers.

In most cases, this original idea filled both a personal need and a market need. It kept the business focused. But as time went on and the business expanded and its leaders changed, the "need" for the business may have gotten fuzzy in the minds of those expected to run it. A business may have a well-developed customer base and an array of products and services, but if it does not understand the needs that the business and its products and services fill, this customer base and the commitment of its people will atrophy over time.

A strategic needs analysis attempts to target precisely:

- Who needs the organization?
- What do these "stakeholders" look to the organization to provide?
- How does the organization meet these needs now?
- What should the organization do to meet these needs in the future?

Often a strategic need analysis begins with a pair of simple questions: "If we were to go out of business tomorrow, who would miss us? Why would they miss us?"

Who would miss your organization—or your HR department—if it ceased to exist tomorrow? Be specific. (Owners, employees, customers, suppliers, members of the community, the media, policymakers, school children, grant recipients...who?)

Why would they miss you? What are they getting from you? Again, be specific. Stockholders might miss you because you represent their life investments and the hopes (for retirement or a college education or a new house) that go with them. Employees might miss you because you provide a paycheck but also because the organization provides them with a sense of belonging and their jobs are important to their self-identities. Why would your customers miss you? Were you providing them with quality goods or cutting-edge information? Was there some cachet in buying your products and services?

Everyone who would miss you if you went out of business is a "customer." In considering why these "customers" would miss you, you need to examine not just their surface needs but also their psychological needs. What do they *hope for* from you?

Different parts of the organization are likely to have different "customers," including internal "customers." Which are high-priority "customers" for the entire organization? Which are high-priority "customers" for various sub-units of the organization? Whose needs should be met first?

Finally, what do you do to help meet these customer needs? What should you consider doing in the future to meet these needs?

A purpose statement should reflect the organization's values, beliefs and priorities as well as how these values, beliefs and priorities will be applied to satisfy, please, even tickle, dazzle and delight the organization's various "customers."

SECTION V WORKSHEET
VISION AND PURPOSE STATEMENTS

Vision and purpose statements should begin with a discussion of the department's core values and guiding philosophies. The following questions should help get the ball rolling.

Why do you dedicate your time and energy to this organization/this department?

_____

_____

_____

What accomplishment here are you proudest of? Why was that important to you?

_____

_____

_____

In your opinion, what are the best things we've done (in the past three years)? Why are these the best things?

_____

_____

_____

If you heard strangers talking about the organization, what are three adjectives you hope they would use? (Why? What do these words mean to you?)

_____

_____

_____

What makes us unique? What do we have to offer that no one else can offer?

_____

_____

_____

What do we contribute to the community/the organization? How does that make a difference?

_____

_____

_____

_____

Why don't we just close down the department?

_____

_____

_____

What do you think this department should look like in five years? Why is that desirable?

_____

_____

_____

Which ideas seem to resonate with your group? Try to distill the essence of these ideas into a brief vision statement. Is your vision statement:

- ✔ compelling, motivational?
- ✔ easily understood?
- ✔ succinct (one or two sentences)?
- ✔ an enduring goal?
- ✔ a view of something different, better?

Purpose statements usually take this discussion of core values and guiding philosophies a step further by applying them to the organization and its stakeholders.

If we were to cease to exist tomorrow, who would miss us?

_____

_____

_____

What do these "stakeholders" look to the department to provide?

_____

_____

_____

How does the department meet these needs now?

_____

_____

_____

What should the department do to meet these needs in the future?

_____

_____

_____

Try distilling these ideas into a purpose statement. Does your purpose statement:

- ✔ support the vision of the department?
- ✔ explain what you do?
- ✔ explain what motivates you to do it?
- ✔ explain who you do it for?
- ✔ reflect the department both as it is *and* as it hopes to become in the future?

SECTION VI
SETTING KEY OBJECTIVES

All of the work you have done to date is brought together in the fourth step of the strategic planning process: setting key objectives.

In the internal and external scans you identified what "is." In the vision and purpose statements you identified what "should be." It is now time to develop a plan for moving the organization from "is" to "should be." This plan has two primary components: the key objectives and the action plan. (See the Appendix for an example of key objectives for an HR department.)

Key objectives are broadly stated goals that the organization considers essential for moving from "is" to "should be."

- Key objectives can be quantitative or qualitative.
- Key objectives can be enduring or specific to a time period.
- Key objectives focus on *what* needs to be accomplished, not *how*.
- Strategic plans rarely have more than five or six key objectives.

Key objectives can be quantitative or qualitative. A quantitative objective might be: "By 1998, our products will be used in 20% of all households in the United States." This objective clearly states what needs to be accomplished, it provides a specific time frame and it sets forth a specific numerical goal.

A qualitative objective might be: "By 1996, the human resource department will be a sought-after and highly regarded resource on employment issues throughout the organization." This objective also clearly states what needs to be accomplished and provides a specific time frame. But, unlike the earlier example, this one focuses on qualitative gains: "sought-after" and "highly regarded" are qualities that are not easily measured. That's not a problem. The purpose of a key objective is to focus the group on a specific issue and set a standard for achievement. Qualitative objectives do this just as effectively as—and sometimes more effectively than—quantitative objectives.

There is an old management saying, "When all you have is a hammer, every problem becomes a nail." Unfortunately, many organizations rely so heavily on quantitative measurements that they ignore or mishandle critical strategic issues that cannot be conveniently reduced to numbers. ("Quality" and "service" are only two examples of strategic issues in which what is measured is often not important and what is important is often not measured.) For those organizations or individuals uncomfortable with qualitative objectives, you may need to give special emphasis to the "signposts for success" (see below).

In each case, an issue that was identified earlier in the strategic planning process—in these two examples, a need for growth or better market penetration and a need to improve internal credibility—is crystallized into a single sentence that lays out a "vision" of the future specific to this issue. Key objectives should always be a "stretch." (Something that people hear and think, "Wow, that's ambitious. But I bet we can do it.")

Key objectives can be enduring or specific to a time period. An enduring objective might be, "Our products will define the industry's state-of-the-art." This is an enduring objective because it does not have an end point: as "state-of-the-art" keeps progressing, so must your efforts. It can remain an objective for as long as the organization chooses to make it one.

An objective specific to a time period might be, "We will outsource our payroll and benefits administration." This objective has an end point. Once you have done it, it stays done unless you choose to undo it. (Note: key objectives need not have dates. Unless otherwise specified, it is assumed all key objectives apply to the years of the planning horizon.)

The scope of your objectives depends on the scope of the organization you are planning for. If you are planning for an entire corporation, it is unlikely that outsourcing payroll and benefits administration would qualify as one of the five or six key strategic concerns of the business. (If important, outsourcing payroll and benefits administration may be listed as an action step somewhere down in the action plan.) If you are doing planning for your HR department, though, this may qualify as one of your five or six key strategic issues. Or it may be an action step under a broader HR key objective like, "Our use of internal and external staff will represent the best mix of expertise and cost-efficiency."

Key objectives focus on what *needs to be accomplished, not* how. Key objectives describe what needs to be done. The action plan describes how and when it will be done and who will do it. (Similarly, the vision and purpose statements describe why it must be.)

In business, as in nature, form should follow function. For this reason, the key objectives—and in fact, the entire planning framework—should focus on *what* an organization does (*e.g.*, provide customers with information), not the various forms the organization has created to do it (*e.g.*, publish reports, host conferences, operate databases). By focusing on the function (what needs to be done) instead of the form (how it will be done), key objectives help ensure that all of the organization's various operating lines are working in concert toward the same goals.

Strategic plans rarely have more than five or six key objectives. This is true for two reasons. First of all, it is difficult for an organization to do more than five or six things well at one time. One of the benefits of strategic planning is concentrating the organization's resources on those things that are most important for getting from "is" to "should be." Second, by limiting itself to five or six key objectives, the organization is forced to set priorities. Of all of the things that the organization must do, or could do, to get from "is" to "should be," which are the five or six most critical?

CHOOSING KEY OBJECTIVES

The key objectives you choose will depend on your organization and what is happening both internally and externally.

In trying to identify key objectives, review your internal and external scans.

- In light of the organization's vision and purpose, what are the internal strengths that should be capitalized on? What are the internal weaknesses that should be shored up?
- In light of the organization's vision and purpose, what are the external threats that the organization should work to minimize? What are the opportunities that the organization should work to develop?

- What are the overall "themes" that emerge from the internal or external scans or the strategic needs analysis?

The key objectives chosen by a given organization will reflect that organization's vision and purpose as well as its own unique internal and external issues. These key objectives should be both necessary and sufficient. In other words, each key objective should be necessary to advance the organization's vision and purpose. (If a key objective is not absolutely necessary, then it shouldn't be a key objective.) Similarly, taken together, the key objectives should be sufficient to achieve the organization's mission or purpose. (If the organization will still fall short of its mission or purpose after all the key objectives are accomplished, the group has not really identified the *key* objectives.)

After your group has chosen its five or six key strategic planning objectives, review them one more time to make sure that (1) they advance the organization's vision and purpose, (2) they represent the most important issues that the organization will need to address to get from "is" to "should be," (3) they are both necessary and sufficient, (4) they focus on what is to be done, not how it is to be done and (5) their wording is clear, concise and captures the spirit of what is to be accomplished.

ESTABLISHING "SIGNPOSTS" FOR SUCCESS

The final step in setting key objectives is developing criteria to determine if the organization is successfully meeting these objectives. These criteria will serve as your plan's "signposts" for success.

Signposts are usually written as events: something that will happen to signal if the organization is making progress toward its objective. They are not a part of the objective—they are simply a sign that things are headed in the right direction.

"Signposts" can be qualitative or quantitative but they must be specific. In the first key objective listed above—"By 1998, our products will be used in 20% of all households in the United States"—a signpost is contained in the objective itself. Your group may want to develop additional signposts for this objective, such as

"One of our products will be mentioned in a major national newspaper at least once a week." Or "The number of positive letters we receive in consumer affairs will increase 30%."

In the second key objective listed above—"By 1996, the human resource department will be a sought-after and highly regarded resource on employment issues throughout the organization"—there is no explicit signpost contained in the objective itself. The group will need to establish some signposts. An example might be "Representatives from the human resource department will be asked to participate in all management decisions affecting the workforce." Or "Line managers will regularly consult with the HR department to solve workplace problems." Or "Employees will encourage each other to go to the HR department for information and assistance with workplace problems."

Signposts serve two primary purposes: on the surface, they are a performance measurement tool, designed to help an organization gauge if it is moving toward its objectives. More implicitly, they are also a means of bringing clarity and purpose to key objectives by further defining and refining the "vision" that is embedded in each key objective.

What does it look like the department should be focusing on during the planning period? Ask your group to nominate candidates for key objectives. Try to group ideas by goal (*e.g.,* improve credibility with senior and line managers) rather than by functional area (*e.g.,* compensation). This will help ensure that the work of the department is focused on key objectives rather than traditional work projects and that the functional areas are working together toward a single objective. (After all, strategic planning should coordinate the work of the department and move it toward a single, agreed-upon end.) You may need to rewrite these key objectives several times until you are confident they:

✓ are complete
✓ represent the department's most critical objectives
✓ focus on *what* needs to happen (not *how* or *by whom*)
✓ are clear, concise and easily understood by anyone who reads them

Try to limit your key objectives to no more than five or six. If you have more than that, you may need to review priorities or the way ideas are grouped together.

List each of your key objectives. What would a "signpost for success" be for each of these objectives? What things might happen to tell you that you are on the right track?

Key Objective 1: _____

Signposts for success:

_____

_____

_____

Key Objective 2: _____

Signposts for success:

_____

_____

_____

Key Objective 3: _____

Signposts for success:

_____

_____

_____

Key Objective 4: _____

   Signposts for success:

_____

_____

_____

Key Objective 5: _____

   Signposts for success:

_____

_____

_____

Key Objective 6: _____

   Signposts for success:

_____

_____

_____

DEVELOPING AN ACTION PLAN

Key objectives provide the basic framework of the strategic plan. They identify *what* must be done. The action plan fills in the details by identifying *how*, *who* and *when*.

The action plan lays out the specific steps necessary to achieve each of the key objectives and assigns timetables and accountability to these steps.

- The action plan can be as detailed as appropriate. Operating like an outline, it can have as many levels of goals as necessary.
- The action plan serves as a means of coordinating and focusing the organization's resources.
- The action plan provides group members with an understanding of how their own work fits into "the big picture."
- The action plan not only says what the organization will do; it also, by implication, says what the organization will *not* do.

Because many organizations use the action plan to develop the next year's budget and operational plan, it should be comprehensive. That said, an action plan should focus the organization's attention on those things necessary to accomplish its key objectives. Actions that are not specifically in support of a key objective should be questioned: why are resources being diverted from those objectives the organization has identified as critical to its future? Just because an organization has "always" done something does not mean it should continue to do it if it no longer advances its goals.

If we use an example, we can examine how an action plan differs from key objectives. Let's say one of the key objectives for your HR department is "Employee training will match or anticipate the skill needs of the company." What steps would be necessary in order to satisfy this objective? Who is going to do them? When they need to be done? A sample "action plan" for this key objective is sketched out below.

Key Objective: Employee training will match or anticipate the skill needs of the company.

    A. Work with department heads, managers and employees to address existing and anticipated skill needs.
        1. Develop a needs assessment to identify existing and anticipated skill requirements and deficiencies: Susan and Steve, by 2/1
        2. Based on the needs assessment, work with managers and employees to develop training plans for specific positions/individuals: Susan and Steve, by 4/15
        3. Begin implementation of training plans as schedules, budgets and priorities permit: HR dept. and managers, by 6/1
        4. Update training plans annually: Steve, Susan and managers by 8/15
    B. Ensure that adequate funding is available in subsequent budget years to fulfill training plans: Janet, annually by 8/15.

All action plans share three characteristics: they should (1) lay out the specific action steps necessary to satisfy a key objective, (2) assign a timetable for the completion of those action steps and (3) indicate who will be responsible for each task. The level of specificity you choose to include in your action plan will depend on the complexity of the objective and how much detail you and your staff or planning group believe is necessary. In all cases, action plans should be specific enough to communicate to superiors, subordinates, peers and anyone else who reads the plan exactly what needs to happen to fulfill the objective and when it needs to happen. Assignments and timetables should be negotiated between the relevant parties *before* the action plan is completed, not merely presented after the fact.

AVOIDING "BUSINESS AS USUAL"

Strategic planning is an opportunity to break away from "business as usual" to examine basic assumptions about the business and to re-think what we do and why we do it. Most organizations do well in this regard until they get to the action temptation of simply squeezing all the activities they are currently doing—or planning to do—into one or another key objective.

To avoid this temptation, ask the group to "brainstorm" options for satisfying each of the key objectives. What are all of the various things the organization could do to satisfy a specific key objective? This approach encourages the group to look beyond what its members are doing now or have done in the past to consider a broader spectrum of possibilities. After the group runs out of ideas, participants can then begin discussing and selecting which of these various options may be the best, given the resources, vision, purpose and objectives of the organization.

Most groups appreciate the value of strategic planning in identifying new projects. Fewer appreciate the value of strategic planning in eliminating old projects. Just because you have "always" done something does not necessarily mean you should continue to do it. Projects that are either no longer necessary to advance the organization's vision and purpose or are no longer the best option for doing so should be abandoned. Some people believe strategic planning leads to *more* work when, in fact, it should lead to *different* work.

Once completed, your action plan should become the basis of your operational plans, budgets and performance appraisals.

SECTION VII WORKSHEET
ACTION PLAN

An action plan is usually in an outline format:

  I. Key Objectives
     A. Goals
       1. Subgoals
         a. Etc.

For each key objective, ask your group to nominate different things the department might be able to do to fulfill each objective. Focus on the best options—which may or may not be the traditional options.

    ✔ What needs to be done? Be specific.
    ✔ Who needs to do it? Cross-functional coordination is important.
    ✔ When does it need to be done? Negotiate timetables, and don't forget: this is probably a multi-year plan.

Resist the temptation to simply jam everything the department is currently doing into one or another key objective. It may help to specifically address what will *not* be done. If you find yourself left with pet projects or other tasks that do not support a key objective, you may need to ask yourself (1) if the key objectives are complete and worded appropriately and (2) if the tasks are really necessary. Because they divert resources from those objectives the group has judged most critical to the future, tasks that do not clearly support a key objective require justification.

Accountability for goals and subgoals should be linked to staff performance measures. Individual and/or group performance measures should explicitly recognize achievement in support of the department's strategic objectives.

EVALUATING PROGRESS

The final step in strategic planning is evaluating progress. All too often, organizations go through the strategic planning process and develop sophisticated plans only to have them sit, untouched, in a binder somewhere. For strategic planning to be an effective tool in moving the organization forward, plans must be implemented and evaluated.

"REALITY CHECKS"

After plan implementation begins, don't sit back and wait a full year to see how the plan is doing. Most organizations build in regular, often quarterly, "reality checks." What's working? What's not? Are there unforeseen problems? Are there unanticipated opportunities? What can the organization do now to make mid-course adjustments?

Like the chess game in the first section of this handbook, the environment in which we live and work is constantly changing. As players, our responses must be dynamic. Events ranging from the unexpected departure of a key employee to a fire or flood can upset our carefully crafted plans. Organizations need to be flexible to survive. This handbook has tried to demonstrate that strategic planning is about more than simply producing a document. It is a process for refreshing and refining our thinking about why the organization exists and what we want the future to look like. It is a process for deciding where we want to go and how we want to get there. As Gen. Dwight D. Eisenhower once observed, "It's not the plan but the planning that counts."

Yet plans that are developed at an off-site retreat and never implemented or never evaluated can feed cynicism about planning. If your organization wants to go through the strategic planning process without committing to the plan, call the exercise something other than strategic planning. If you do intend to implement the plan, progress should be monitored through regular "reality checks" to ensure the plan is on track and to permit the organization to adjust course as necessary to take advantage of changing circumstances.

IMPROVING AND RENEWING THE PROCESS

Each time you journey through the strategic planning process, you no doubt will discover areas that you can improve upon for next time. And there will be a next time. While the vision of the organization is unlikely to change with any regularity, virtually everything else will change: internal resources and capabilities, the external environment, the organization's definition of its purpose, its key objective and its action plan.

How often you choose to undertake the entire strategic planning process will depend in large part on your organization. Many organizations choose to do strategic planning annually, creating a "rolling" strategic plan with a planning horizon that always extends two, three, five or more years into the future. Other organizations update parts of the plan annually but go through the entire process only every two or three years. Your decision will depend on your organization's needs and the speed at which both the organization and its external environment are changing.

For many groups, one of the most difficult aspects of strategic planning is coming to the process fresh each time. People tend to assume that the world of last year or two years ago, when they last did strategic planning, is pretty much the same as the world is now. In a sense it is: although you may encounter a few "wildcards" that you did not anticipate last year, the basic elements of this year were probably present last year. The difference is the arrangement of the elements and their meaning for the organization. In fact, the various facets of the organization and its environment can be likened to the pieces of glass in a kaleidoscope: coming together to create a coherent whole, only to break apart and create a new whole when the situation changes. Consequently, plans and their underlying assumptions need to be revisited and updated regularly, even when it appears at first glance that nothing is particularly new or different.

Done well, strategic planning can be a powerful tool for moving an organization toward its preferred future and, as such, should be part of every human resource professional's toolbox.

SECTION VIII WORKSHEET
EVALUATING PROGRESS

A strategic plan should be evaluated regularly to confirm that the plan itself is still sound and that implementation is on target.

What are the unforeseen problems?

_____

_____

_____

What are the unforeseen opportunities?

_____

_____

_____

Can—and should—the department adjust its plan in light of these unforeseen problems and/or opportunities?**

_____

_____

_____

> ***Don't let every unforeseen problem and opportunity push you "off plan." Any adjustments you make should be consistent with the department's vision, purpose and key objectives.*

Is implementation of the plan on target? Where is it ahead of or behind schedule?

_____

_____

_____

What have you learned from this experience? What would you like to do better or differently next time?

_____

_____

_____

A Sample Strategic Planning "Shell" for the HR Department

Vision

To improve the lives of our employees and our stockholders by building a workplace based on mutual trust, respect and enlightened human resource management practices.

Purpose

The HR department is committed to creating competitive advantage for XYZ Corp. by providing innovative, cost-effective solutions to human resource management problems.

Key Objectives

I. The human resource department will be a sought-after resource on employment issues throughout the organization.

II. The HR department will work closely with employees, line supervisors and senior management to ensure that the skills of XYZ employees meet the present and future needs of XYZ Corp.

III. XYZ's reward systems will be closely linked to individual and team performance in support of XYZ's business objectives.

IV. The HR department will design and maintain an employee benefits program that cost-effectively meets the diverse needs of the XYZ workforce.

V. The HR department's use of internal and external resources will represent the best mix of expertise and value.

BIOGRAPHIES

Christine D. Keen is a principal and founding partner of The Domani Group, an international research and consulting firm based in Washington, DC, specializing in emerging issues and their strategic implications for business and public policy. A frequent writer and speaker, Ms. Keen is considered a leading-edge analyst of the forces transforming business and society. Her work focuses on helping organizations anticipate—and capitalize on—future change.

Prior to joining The Domani Group in 1992, Ms. Keen directed the award-winning issues management program at the Society for Human Resource Management and served as a trend analyst with The Naisbitt Group, the future forecasting firm founded by *Megatrends* author John Naisbitt.

Ms. Keen is the former editor of the newsletter *Issues in HR*, and her insights about the future have appeared in such publications as *The Wall Street Journal*, *Vital Speeches of the Day*, *HR Magazine*, *Futures Research Quarterly*, *Association Trends*, *Executive Speaker* and *HR Horizons*, as well as having been selected for broadcast on "Voice of America." She is an honors graduate of Dartmouth College and holds an M.A. in public policy from George Washington University.

Michael R. Losey, SPHR, President & CEO of the Society for Human Resource Management (SHRM), formerly the American Society for Personnel Administration (ASPA), has 30 years' experience in all areas of human resource management. As President and Chief Executive Officer of SHRM, Losey oversees all organizational, operational and strategic planning for the Society.

Before being named to the Society's top administrative position in 1990, Losey served more than 28 years in management and executive level positions with two Fortune 50 organizations.

As a member of SHRM, Losey has been involved at the national level as a member of the Legislative Affairs Committee and at the local level as a member of the SHRM Greater Valley Forge (PA) Personnel Association. He has also been active in international human resources and has recently been elected to the position of Secretary General of the World Federation of Personnel Management Associations (WFPMA)—a worldwide organization of human resource professional organizations in more than 50 countries. In addition to serving on the SHRM Board of Directors and boards of the Human Resource Certification Institute and the SHRM Foundation, he is a Fellow of the National Academy of Human Resources, an honor considered one of the most prestigious in the human resource field.

Losey holds both bachelor's and master's degrees of Business Administration in Industrial Relations from the University of Michigan. He is a frequent speaker, author and spokesperson for SHRM on human resource management issues to the SHRM membership, other organizations, international media and Congress. Mr. Losey is a certified Senior Professional in Human Resources (SPHR).

Losey represents the interests of the Society's membership, which currently stands at more than 60,000 members in 44 countries and more than 430 professional and 300 student chapters.